TEMPERATURES

°F (Fahrenheit)	°C (Celsius)
32	
200	
212	
250	
300	
350 (r	
400 (h	
450 (ve	
500 (ext	

LENGTHS

U.S. Measurements	Metric Equivalents
¼ inch	6 mm
½ inch	1.2 cm
¾ inch	2 cm
1 inch	2.5 cm
2 inches	5 cm
5 inches	12.5 cm

LITTLE BOOKS FOR COOKS
GARLIC

LITTLE BOOKS FOR COOKS

GARLIC

ANDREWS AND MCMEEL
A UNIVERSAL PRESS SYNDICATE COMPANY
KANSAS CITY

LITTLE BOOKS FOR COOKS: GARLIC copyright © 1997 by Smallwood and Stewart, Inc. All rights reserved. Printed in Hong Kong. No part of this book may be used or reproduced in any manner whatsoever without written permission except in the case of reprints in the context of reviews. For information write Andrews and McMeel, a Universal Press Syndicate Company, 4520 Main Street, Kansas City, Missouri 64111.

ISBN: 0-8362-2777-8
Library of Congress Catalog Card Number: 96-86647

First U.S. edition
1 3 5 7 9 10 8 6 4 2

Editor: Deri Reed
Designer: Yolanda Monteza
Photographer: Steven Mark Needham
Illustrator: Ed Lam

Produced by Smallwood and Stewart, Inc., New York City

TABLE OF CONTENTS

INTRODUCTION
6

TYPES OF GARLIC
12

GARLIC TIPS
23

RECIPES
26

G A R L

In ancient times, it was thought to repel vampires and other evil spirits, along with curing fever, consumption, toothache, snakebite, and the plague. In the 19th century, it was said to cure the vapors and was used as an antiseptic and antibiotic, applied directly to wounds and infections. Today, studies show that it may lower cholesterol, thin blood, lower blood pressure, help prevent cancer, boost the immune system, and ward off cold and flu viruses.

It's garlic, and it's been both reviled and

I C

adored (it isn't nicknamed "the stinking rose" for nothing) by different cultures for thousands of years. Even just 20 years ago, garlic had a humble image, and was disparaged as "peasant food." But now that we've started to appreciate its gusto and sweet mellowness, its piquant aroma, its healthfulness and most of all its versatility, garlic has become the darling of home cooks and chefs alike.

There isn't a time when garlic wasn't a part of the world's cuisines. The speculation is that garlic is native to central Asia, as there are records of ancient Chinese using it. Mention is made in the Old Testament of the Jews missing the garlic (and onions and leeks) of Egypt. Ancient Egyptian tombs have depictions of garlic, as does the Great Pyramid of Giza. Early Roman laborers and soldiers ate garlic for strength and courage, but the nobles wouldn't touch it, as it was considered somewhat low-brow.

Pungent and biting in a quick stir-fry or sweet and mellow after a long, slow roast, versatile garlic will spice up or complement almost every food it encounters. Of course, we know that Italian and French cooks love garlic, but it's very popular in Spanish, Mexican, Asian, Eastern European, and Middle Eastern cuisines, too. Garlic takes the starring role in sauces like France's *aïoli, rouille* and *pistou;* Tunisia's *harissa,* and Italy's *pesto*. And let's not forget the many other classic dishes that simply wouldn't exist without garlic: *bourride,* the creamy garlicky fish soup from France; Spain's garlic soup; spinach stir-fry with garlic from China; and American garlic mashed potatoes.

GARLIC AND YOUR HEALTH

The ancients always thought garlic was good for your health; now, modern science is proving it. Medical research has shown that garlic can:

- Protect the heart by lowering blood cholesterol and triglycerides, thinning the blood, lowering blood pressure, and increasing circulation.
- Enhance the immune system by increasing activity of immune cells.
- Protect the nervous system by providing anti-aging effects.
- Ward off infections by killing the yeast *candida* and other bacteria.

- Assist in preventing cancer by inhibiting the formation of cancer-causing compounds and decreasing side effects of cancer drugs.
- Protect the body from toxins.

Further information is available from the Garlic Information Center at The New York Hospital-Cornell University Medical Center (telephone (800) 330-5922). Their studies indicate that garlic supplements such as garlic oil or aged garlic extract have the same healthy benefits as regular garlic (though we think: why miss out on all that great garlic taste?) and, in good news for cooks, that cooking garlic does not decrease its potency.

TYPES OF

GARLIC

AMERICAN: This is the common white garlic, with creamy white cloves and a strong flavor. Inexpensive and readily available year round, it is a staple in most kitchens.

MEXICAN and ITALIAN: The milder, purple cousins to American garlic, available in gourmet stores and larger supermarkets. Use as you would regular garlic, but expect a little less punch in flavor.

ELEPHANT: Huge heads of garlic with large cloves that peel easily and are very mild in flavor. Elephant garlic is not true garlic, but instead is more closely related to leeks (though the flavor is more like garlic than leek).

GREEN GARLIC: The immature garlic plant with unformed cloves and very mild flavor. Green garlic looks like a scallion with a lumpy bulb near the root end. Use as you would regular garlic, but expect a milder, distinctive flavor. Only occasionally available in specialty stores and farmers' markets, grab green garlic when you can. Store in a plastic bag in the refrigerator for up to a week.

BUYING GARLIC

Look for compact heads with plump firm bulbs, dry skin, and no soft or brown spots; avoid garlic that has sprouted or heads that come apart too easily (this means the garlic is past fresh and losing moisture and essential oils).

GARLIC TIPS

To peel garlic, whack a clove with the side of a knife and then slice off the root end; the skin should slide right off. If you have a lot of cloves to peel, submerge them in boiling water 30 seconds, refresh in cold water, and peel.

Puréeing, mincing, or chopping garlic releases more of the essential oils, and therefore makes the garlic more potent than slicing or leaving the cloves whole.

When mincing or puréeing garlic with a knife, sprinkle the garlic with a big pinch of salt; it will help extract the juices and keep your knife clean.

To soften the punch of garlic, some cooks like to remove the germ or "lily" inside the clove (which produces the sprout in older garlic): Cut the clove in half and gently lift out the germ with the tip of the knife. Another taming trick: Parboil whole cloves for 30 to 60 seconds before slicing, mincing, or cooking whole.

Be sure not to allow garlic to brown when sautéing — it turns bitter and acrid.

Most food experts eschew the garlic press: Aside from the fact that cleaning it is very difficult, the metal reacts with the garlic and gives it an "off" taste. For the same reason, many cooks don't chop garlic in a food processor or blender.

To grow garlic chives in your kitchen: Plant individual garlic cloves ½" apart in pots, with just the pointy ends poking out. Soon they'll sprout garlic chives. Snip them as you would regular chives and add to soups, salads, or stir-fries.

How to get rid of garlic breath: The time-honored remedy is to chew on parsley sprigs, but you can also try chewing on a coffee bean or fennel seeds. A citrus sorbet might help alleviate the problem as well.

And to get the smell off your hands, rub with lemon juice or the cut side of lemon and salt, then wash with soap and warm water.

R E C I

P E S

Roasted Garlic

Remove only the outer loose, papery skins from a head of garlic, keeping the head whole; cut 1/4" to 1/2" off the top to expose the cloves. Drizzle with olive oil and sprinkle with your favorite herb (rosemary and thyme work well, but try others). Then loosely wrap the garlic in foil or place in a clay garlic roaster and cover. Roast in a 350°F oven 30 to 45 minutes, until the cloves are soft. Let cool slightly and squeeze the pulp out of the skins.

The slightly nutty, sweet garlic is delicious on bread. But also try it on grilled meat or fish, mixed into mashed potatoes, and as a topping on baked potatoes. Or, you can rub it under the skin of chicken before roasting.

Aïoli

Aïoli, the pungent garlic mayonnaise, is practically a staple in parts of France. It's most popular as a key flavoring ingredient in the fish soup *Bourride* (page 42), but the French also smear aïoli on roasted chicken and broiled fish and use it as a dip for crudites. If you prefer an aïoli with lots of garlic taste but less bite, roast the garlic first.

AÏOLI

6 garlic cloves, minced
¼ teaspoon salt
2 large egg yolks
1 cup extra virgin olive oil
2 tablespoons lemon juice

Caution:

The salmonella bacteria from infected, uncooked eggs can cause serious food poisoning. We recommend using eggs only from organic, free-range hens and washing the eggs thoroughly before breaking their shells. We don't recommend serving raw egg to the very old, the very young, or anyone with a compromised immune system.

In a small bowl, using the back of a spoon or with a mortar and pestle, mash the garlic and salt to make a smooth paste. Stir in the egg yolks, then whisk in half of the olive oil, drop by drop, until it has been incorporated. Add the lemon juice and whisk in the remaining olive oil until the mixture is glossy and the consistency of mayonnaise.

Serve with roasted chicken, steamed potatoes, and a variety of steamed vegetables. *Makes about 2 ¼ cups.*

Quick Aïoli

For a fast, no-fuss, salmonella-free garlic mayonnaise, combine ¾ cup of store-bought mayonnaise with 1 tablespoon olive oil, 1 tablespoon lemon juice, and 1 tablespoon puréed garlic. Serve with lamb, pork, chicken, or fish.

Pesto

This garlic-spiked green sauce from Genoa, Italy, is a popular pasta coating. But you can also add a spoonful to salad dressings and marinades. Or mix a little into mayonnaise to brighten up sandwiches and dribble over thick slices of summer tomatoes.

PESTO

2 cups packed fresh basil leaves
1 cup fresh flat-leaf parsley
4 garlic cloves
1/4 cup toasted pine nuts or walnuts
1/2 teaspoon salt
Freshly ground black pepper, to taste
1/2 to 3/4 cup extra virgin olive oil
1/2 cup grated Parmesan cheese

In a food processor, combine the basil, parsley, and garlic; pulse several times to blend. Add the pine nuts or walnuts, salt, and pepper. With the motor running, drizzle in enough olive oil to make a thick sauce. Remove pesto to a small bowl and stir in the Parmesan. Store in the refrigerator, covered with a thin layer of olive oil, in a jar with a tight-fitting lid. *Makes about 1 cup.*

Provençal Vegetable Soup with Pistou

Pistou, the French version of pesto, has lots of garlic like its Italian cousin, but no pine nuts. This soup, a Provençal version of minestrone, is full of vegetables and hearty enough to be enjoyed as a main dish. Note that the *pistou* should not be heated, but added to the soup just before it goes to the table.

PROVENÇAL VEGETABLE SOUP WITH PISTOU

- 2 tablespoons olive oil
- 1 large onion, chopped
- 2 medium leeks, rinsed and thinly sliced
- 3 garlic cloves, thinly sliced
- 3 fresh ripe medium tomatoes, chopped
- 1 medium carrot, halved lengthwise and thinly sliced
- 1 cup cooked white cannellini beans
- 2 teaspoons salt
- 1 cup green beans, cut into 1" lengths
- 1 medium zucchini, halved lengthwise and thinly sliced
- 3/4 cup uncooked elbow macaroni

Pistou:

- 3 garlic cloves, chopped
- 1/4 teaspoon salt
- 1/4 cup lightly packed fresh basil leaves
- 1/3 cup grated Parmesan cheese
- 3 tablespoons extra virgin olive oil

In a Dutch oven, heat the olive oil over medium-low heat. Add the onion and cook, stirring occasionally, 7 minutes, until soft. Add the leeks and garlic and cook 2 minutes. Add 10 cups of water, the tomatoes, carrot, white beans, and salt. Bring to a boil over medium-high heat; reduce the heat to low and simmer 30 minutes. Add the green beans, zucchini, and macaroni, and simmer 15 minutes.

Meanwhile, prepare the *pistou:* Using the back of a spoon or with a mortar and pestle, mash the garlic and salt to make a smooth paste. Add the basil and pound until well combined. Transfer to a small bowl. Add the Parmesan and olive oil and beat until creamy.

To serve, remove the soup from the heat and stir in the pistou. *Serves 8.*

Bourride

This French classic, a hearty, creamy fish soup, is for garlic-lovers only, as the aïoli is incorporated directly into the soup. Use a mixture of firm-fleshed white fish: Halibut, flounder, cod, snapper, and bass are good choices.

BOURRIDE

- 1/2 cup dry white wine
- 2 1/2 pounds bones from any white-fleshed fish, cut into large pieces
- 1 large onion, thinly sliced
- 1 large leek, rinsed and thinly sliced
- 1 large carrot, thinly sliced
- 1 celery stalk, thinly sliced
- 2 sprigs fresh thyme
- 1 bay leaf
- Two (3" x 1/2") strips orange zest
- 1/2 teaspoon fennel seeds
- 1/2 teaspoon salt
- 1 pound all-purpose potatoes, peeled and thinly sliced
- 2 1/2 pounds assorted firm-fleshed white fish, skin left on and cut into large chunks
- 1 recipe for Aïoli, page 30
- 2 large egg yolks
- Snipped fresh chives and julienned carrot and cucumber, for garnish

In a stockpot over medium-high heat, combine 10 cups water with the wine, fish bones, onion, leek, carrot, celery, thyme, bay leaf, orange zest, fennel seeds, and salt. Bring to a boil, reduce the heat, and simmer, skimming off any scum that rises to the surface, for 45 minutes. Strain the stock and discard the solids.

Return the stock to the pot and bring to a boil over high heat. Add the potatoes and cook 5 minutes. Reduce the heat to medium-low, add the fish, and simmer 10 minutes, until the fish is just cooked. With a slotted spoon, transfer the fish and potatoes to a platter and keep warm.

In a medium bowl, whisk together ¾ cup of the aïoli and the egg yolks. Gradually whisk in ½ cup of the stock. Whisk the aïoli mixture back into the stock in the pot and cook over low heat (just under a simmer) for 3 to 4 minutes, until thick and creamy; do not allow the mixture to boil. Place the fish and potatoes in 8 warm soup bowls and ladle the stock on top. Garnish with chives, carrot, and cucumber. Serve with the remaining aïoli and toasted bread slices on the side. *Serves 8.*

Garlic Soup

A traditional Spanish peasant dish, this soup relies upon the most basic ingredients: water, garlic, and bread. Here, we embellish it a bit with chicken stock and ham, but without losing the essence of the garlic flavor.

GARLIC SOUP

- 7 cups chicken stock
- 2 beef bones
- 1 garlic head, separated into cloves, unpeeled, plus 8 garlic cloves, peeled and chopped
- 4 fresh parsley sprigs
- Salt and freshly ground black pepper, to taste
- 1 tablespoon olive oil
- 1/4 pound cured ham, such as prosciutto, sliced 1/4" thick and diced
- 1 tablespoon paprika
- 1/2 teaspoon ground cumin
- 8 Italian or French bread slices, toasted and brushed with olive oil

In a large saucepan, combine the stock, bones, garlic head, parsley, salt, and pepper. Bring to a boil, reduce the heat to medium, and simmer, uncovered, for 30 minutes. Strain into another saucepan and discard the solids. (You should have about 6 cups soup.)

Meanwhile, heat the olive oil in a medium skillet over medium heat and sauté the chopped garlic 8 to 10 minutes, until lightly golden. Add the ham and cook 1 minute more. Stir in the paprika and cumin and remove from the heat. Add the garlic mixture to the soup and bring to a simmer. Simmer gently for 5 minutes.

Serve with toasted bread directly in the soup.

Serves 4.

Garlic and Citrus Olive Oil

Drizzle this oil over fish, lamb, or chicken before sautéing or grilling, or use in a stir-fry or a vinaigrette.

In a quart bottle with a tight-fitting lid, combine several peeled and quartered cloves of garlic, the zest of 2 lemons and 1 orange, and 2 teaspoons of toasted fennel seeds. Pour in extra virgin olive oil to cover. Cap tightly and let stand at room temperature, occasionally shaking gently, for 2 or 3 days. Strain the oil well, and store in decorative jars with a strip of lemon peel in each. The oil will keep for a week, tightly covered in the refrigerator.

Stir-Fried Spinach with Fragrant Garlic

This quick Chinese stir-fry takes advantage of the simplest, freshest ingredients. If you can, use young spinach with its pink roots and tender stems still attached. Look for it in loose bunches in Chinese produce markets. Otherwise, choose loose spinach, not the prepackaged variety, and remove the roots.

STIR-FRIED SPINACH WITH FRAGRANT GARLIC

- **1 pound baby spinach with pink roots**
- **3 to 5 tablespoons vegetable oil**
- **7 garlic cloves, smashed and peeled**
- **1 teaspoon salt**
- **1 teaspoon sugar**

Rinse the spinach carefully, but do not cut off pink roots or stems. Drain well.

Heat a wok or large skillet over high heat until it just begins to smoke. Add 3 tablespoons of the oil and the garlic and cook for 1 minute. Add the spinach and stir-fry rapidly for 2 to 3 minutes, until the leaves begin to soften. Cover the wok and cook the spinach mixture over medium-high heat for 1 minute more. Uncover, stir in the salt, sugar, and if the spinach seems dry, the remaining 2 tablespoons oil. Continue to stir-fry rapidly until the spinach is limp. Serve immediately. *Serves 4 to 6.*

Catalan
Country Bread

This tomato-dressed version of garlic bread is from the Catalonia region of Spain. As an appetizer, it is often topped with a thin slice of cured ham or with anchovy fillets. Because of its simplicity, the ingredients must be the best: crusty bread, flavorful olive oil, and vine-ripened tomatoes. Serve with Clams with Garlic and White Wine (page 58).

CATALAN COUNTRY BREAD

6 bread slices, 1/2" thick, from a large round loaf

2 large garlic cloves, halved

2 fresh ripe juicy tomatoes, halved

Extra virgin olive oil, to taste

Coarse salt, to taste

Preheat the oven to 350°F. Arrange the bread slices on a baking sheet and bake 8 to 10 minutes, until lightly toasted on both sides. Let cool.

Rub the cut side of a garlic clove over both sides of each bread slice. Then rub the bread on both sides with the cut sides of the tomatoes, squeezing each tomato half slightly to release its juice. Drizzle with the olive oil and sprinkle with salt. *Serves 6.*

Clams with Garlic and White Wine

Be sure to serve a lot of good crusty bread (or Catalan Country Bread, page 54) with this garlicky appetizer, in order to mop up all the sauce. The clams should be the smallest available—ideally littlenecks or cockles. (Pictured on page 55.)

- 2 dozen small clams, thoroughly scrubbed
- 1 tablespoon cornmeal or flour
- 3 tablespoons olive oil
- 1/4 cup minced onion
- 3 garlic cloves, minced
- 1/2 cup dry white wine
- 1/4 cup fish stock or clam juice
- 1 tablespoon lemon juice
- 1 bay leaf
- 3 tablespoons minced fresh parsley
- Freshly ground black pepper, to taste

CLAMS WITH GARLIC AND WHITE WINE

Put the clams in a bowl, cover with salted cold water, and sprinkle with cornmeal. Refrigerate, uncovered, several hours or overnight to rid the clams of sand.

Drain, rinse, and dry the clams. Heat the olive oil in a large, shallow flameproof casserole over high heat and sauté the onion and garlic 4 to 5 minutes, until softened. Just before the garlic browns, add the clams and cook, stirring, about 3 minutes. Add the wine and let it cook off.

Stir in the stock, lemon juice, bay leaf, 1 tablespoon of the parsley, and the pepper. Reduce heat to medium, cover, and cook, removing clams as they open to a warm platter; add a little water if the liquid evaporates before all the clams have opened. (The finished dish should have some sauce.) Discard the bay leaf and any clams that do not open. Return the opened clams to the casserole, heat 1 minute, and sprinkle with the remaining parsley. *Serves 6.*

Spaghettini with Garlic, Olive Oil, and Ginger

Adding fresh ginger to the classic combination of spaghetti, olive oil, and garlic gives this pasta a distinctive flavor. Serve as an appetizer or side dish, or top with grilled shrimp for a quick no-fuss dinner.

- 1/2 cup olive oil
- 1/2 cup minced fresh parsley
- 4 large garlic cloves, minced
- 1 tablespoon minced fresh ginger root
- 1 1/2 tablespoons salt
- 1/8 teaspoon freshly ground black pepper
- 1 pound thin spaghetti

Heat the olive oil in a large skillet over medium-high heat. Stir in the parsley, garlic, and ginger, and immediately remove the pan from the heat. Add ½ teaspoon of the salt and the pepper and allow the mixture to steep; set aside.

Bring several quarts of water to a boil and stir in the remaining salt. Add the pasta and cook until just done, 4 to 5 minutes, or according to package directions. Drain the pasta, add to the sauce in the skillet, and toss to coat well. *Serves 4.*

Warm Garlic–New Potato Salad

Roasted garlic and olive oil make a delicious dressing in this new take on an old standby. Red-skinned new potatoes are the best choice because they keep their shape and texture when cooked and quartered.

WARM GARLIC–NEW POTATO SALAD

- 10 garlic cloves
- 2 pounds red new potatoes
- 1 tablespoon salt
- 2 tablespoons extra virgin olive oil
- 1 tablespoon balsamic vinegar
- 1 teaspoon minced fresh parsley
- 1 teaspoon minced fresh marjoram
- 1 teaspoon fresh rosemary leaves, crumbled
- 1 teaspoon minced fresh thyme
- 1/2 teaspoon freshly ground black pepper

Preheat the oven to 400°F. Wrap the garlic in foil or place in a clay garlic roaster and cover. Bake for 30 minutes, until soft. When cool enough to handle, squeeze out the pulp and set aside; discard the skins.

Meanwhile, in a large saucepan, combine the potatoes with enough water to cover by 3 inches. Add 2 teaspoons of the salt and bring to a boil over high heat. Reduce the heat to medium and cook, uncovered, for 15 minutes, until the potatoes are just tender when pierced with a fork. Drain well. When cool enough to handle, cut the potatoes into quarters, transfer to a baking pan large enough to hold all of them in a single layer, and set aside.

In a food processor, combine the roasted garlic pulp, olive oil, vinegar, and the remaining salt; process until puréed. Pour the garlic mixture over the potatoes and toss to coat.

Bake for 15 minutes. Sprinkle with the parsley, marjoram, rosemary, thyme, and pepper and toss to coat. Bake for another 5 to 10 minutes, until the potatoes begin to turn golden. Allow to cool slightly and serve warm. *Serves 6.*

Garlic Mashed Potatoes

This is a simply heavenly (i.e., garlicky) version of the most traditional American potato dish. For best results, use Yellow Finn potatoes, which are grown in the Pacific Northwest and available in specialty produce markets.

GARLIC MASHED POTATOES

2½ pounds Yellow Finn or Idaho potatoes, peeled and quartered

2 large garlic heads, cloves separated and peeled

¼ cup (½ stick) unsalted butter, softened

½ cup half-and-half, warmed

Salt and white pepper, to taste

Bring a large saucepan of salted water to a boil over high heat. Add the potatoes and garlic, reduce the heat to medium-high, and boil gently, uncovered, for about 20 minutes, until the potatoes and garlic are tender. Drain well and reserve ½ cup of the cooking liquid.

Transfer the potatoes and garlic to a large bowl. Add the butter and coarsely mash the potatoes and garlic with a potato masher or fork. Make a well in the center of the potatoes and pour in the warm half-and-half. Using a handheld electric mixer, beat the mixture just until light and creamy. If necessary, add some of the reserved cooking liquid to achieve a smooth, fluffy texture. Season with salt and pepper and serve immediately. *Serves 6.*

Garlic Shrimp

In Spain this is a favorite *tapa,* or appetizer, served sizzling hot in shallow earthenware casserole bowls. Good crusty bread is a must for dunking in the sauce.

GARLIC SHRIMP

- 3/4 pound small shrimp, shelled
- Salt, to taste
- 1/4 cup olive oil
- 4 garlic cloves, sliced
- 1 small dried red chile pepper, seeds removed and cut in half, or 1/4 teaspoon crushed red pepper flakes
- 1 tablespoon lemon juice
- 1 tablespoon dry white wine
- 2 tablespoons minced fresh parsley

Sprinkle the shrimp with salt. In a shallow flame-proof casserole over medium-high heat, heat the olive oil, garlic, and chile pepper or pepper flakes. When the garlic is just beginning to brown, add the shrimp and cook, stirring, about 1 minute, until just done and firm to the touch. Stir in the lemon juice, wine, and parsley and serve immediately. *Serves 4 to 6.*

Chicken in Garlic Sauce

Garlic takes a starring role in this Spanish dish that's as tasty as it is simple to make. Typically, it is cooked and served in an earthenware casserole, but you can also use a heavy covered skillet.

CHICKEN IN GARLIC SAUCE

One 3-pound chicken, cut into 8 pieces

Salt, to taste

5 tablespoons olive oil

6 garlic cloves, chopped, plus 1 clove, minced

1 tablespoon minced fresh parsley

2 tablespoons dry white wine

Sprinkle the chicken with salt. Heat the olive oil in a shallow flameproof casserole and brown the chicken over medium-high heat on all sides. Add the chopped garlic, reduce the heat to medium, and cook, stirring occasionally, for 30 minutes. Stir in the minced garlic, parsley, and wine. Cover and cook for 15 minutes more, until the chicken is done and the juices run clear when a thigh is pricked with a fork. *Serves 4.*

Garlic and Dill Vinegar

Use this vinegar to brighten a sauce, marinade, or vinaigrette.

In a large glass jar, place several peeled cloves of garlic. Pack in a handful of fresh dill sprigs that have been thoroughly washed. Add one tablespoon of pickling spice and a few black peppercorns, then fill with white or rice wine vinegar. Let stand at room temperature for 3 days, turning the jar often to stir the mixture. Strain well and pour into decorative jars with a fresh sprig of dill in each. Refrigerate for up to 6 months.